Theresa

Pete

Chrissie

Morpho

rfly
dren

DC

Claudette

Cleo

Chuku

ISBN. 978-1-9999545-0-5

Printed in the UK • Published by The Butterfly Children Limited

The Butterfly Children

WHIZZING THROUGH THE WOODS

CREATED BY ANGELA KINCAID

Story by
The Butterfly Children

Illustrated by
Angela Kincaid

Rudy

eep in the woods where people seldom go
live The Butterfly Children.

It was early morning and The Butterfly Children were asleep.
All of a sudden DC was woken up by a loud crashing and
banging that echoed through the woods. DC rubbed his
eyes and stretched his wings.

"Who's making that noise?" he said looking around.
DC thought that he had better have a look so he flew out
of his flower to investigate.

It was Rudy putting the wheel on his new cart.

"I couldn't wait to finish it." he said

"Sorry if I woke everyone up DC."

"Finished." he said "You can have the first go if you like?"

"Really." said DC.

Rudy jumped into the cart and handed DC the rope.

"Start pulling" he said.

"I might have known there was a catch" said DC

as he began to pull Rudy along the path.

"Faster, Faster!" shouted Rudy.

After a while DC had to stop to catch his breath,
he looked up and saw Theresa brushing her hair.
"Looks like fun." she said.
"It's not for girls." said Rudy.
"It's too fast for girls, come on DC let's get going."
DC took a deep breath and off they went again even faster.

As they were whizzing through the woods they nearly knocked Chrissie over.

"Beep, Beep!" yelled Rudy. "Out of the way, stand back, this is not for girls!"

"Look where you're going!" Chrissie shouted.

Rudy tugged even harder on the rope.

"Come on DC, faster, faster!" he shouted.

Soon DC became very tired and had to stop and sit down.

"I'm puffed out, I can't go another step." he said.

Rudy moaned, "Who's going to pull my cart now?" he said.

Just then Susie flew down.

"Wow, what a great cart can I have a go?"

she said sitting in the cart with Rudy.

"No, it's not for girls, girls can't pull carts." said Rudy.

"But I know someone who can." said Susie.

She whistled loudly and out popped a brown Rabbit.

Susie tied the rope round Rabbit and whispered in his ear.

Rudy looked a little worried, what was she saying to him?

"You want to go fast, well hang on to your hat!"

Susie jumped into the cart and whistled loudly, and they were off!

Rabbit ran a lot faster than DC and Rudy had to hold on tight.

"AAAGHHH!" screamed Rudy as the cart went whizzing
through the woods.

"Slow down, Slow down!" he cried, but Susie and Rabbit
did not hear him shouting.

DC and Chrissie were flying as fast as they could in front of them,
but they didn't hear DC shouting.

"Stop! Stop!" he cried as they crashed into the log laying on the path.

Susie and Rudy were thrown to the ground.

"Sorry Susie" said Rudy "It's those Moths again,
they always cause trouble."
DC and Chrissie looked around.
"It's not the Moths, it's just an accident, a branch has
fallen off the tree in the wind." said DC.
"I think Rabbit and Susie have taught Rudy a lesson
about going too fast." he said.
"And not looking where they were going." added Chrissie,
and they all laughed.

Deep in the woods where people seldom go.
Carting can be fun.

Hawkeye

Dogstooth

Blackneck

Moth

Drab